IMAGINED GREETINGS

By the same author:

Warriors
(Poetry) Salt Publications

The Gospel According to Frank
(Poetry) New American Press

Other Land: Contemporary Poems on Wales and Welsh-American Experience
(Poetry anthology) Parthian Press

Boys: Stories and a Novella
(Short fiction) Syracuse University Press

The Everyday Apocalypse
(Poetry) Three Conditions Press

Writing on the Edge: Interviews with Writers and Editors of Wales
(Interviews) Rodopi

The Urgency of Identity: Contemporary English-Language Poetry from Wales
(Poetry anthology with interviews)
TriQuarterly Books/Northwestern University Press

Over the Line
(Novel) Syracuse University Press

Imagined Greetings

*Poetic Engagements with
R. S. Thomas*

David Lloyd (ed.)

First published in 2013

© Text: David Lloyd/Gwasg Carreg Gwalch 2013
© prose and poems: original rights

All rights reserved. No part of this publication
may be reproduced, stored in a retrieval system,
or transmitted in any form or by any means, electronic,
electrostatic, magnetic tape, mechanical, photocopying,
recording, or otherwise, without prior permission
of the authors of the works herein.

Published with the financial support
of the Welsh Books Council

ISBN: 978-1-84527-416-0

Cover design: Welsh Books Council

Published by Gwasg Carreg Gwalch,
12 Iard yr Orsaf, Llanrwst, Wales LL26 0EH
tel: 01492 624031
fax: 01492 641502
email: books@carreg-gwalch.com
internet: www.carreg-gwalch.com

for my sister, Margaret Glynne Lloyd

and for John K. Bollard

Contents

Foreword: Gareth Neigwl	9
Introduction	13
Dannie Abse: Is Creation a Destructive Force?	21
Myrddin ap Dafydd: Awyren uwch angladd R.S.	22
Roy Ashwell: R.S. Writes his Biography in a New Tongue	24
Bryan Aspden: Travellers In The Dream Trade	25
Ruth Bidgood: Bereft	27
Jane Blank: R. S. Thomas in Eglwys Fach	28
Gillian Clarke: RS	30
Tony Conran: The Great R.S. is Gone	31
John Davies: R. S. Thomas	32
William Virgil Davis: First Light	34
The Island	35
Jon Dressel: Dai, Live	36
Note to a Character	38
Dai on Holiday	39
Dai Communicates	40
Dim Cyffesu	41
Cân Rhyfelwr	42
Menna Elfyn: Y Bardd Di-flewyn	44
Cusan Hances	48
Titw Tomos	50
Peter Finch: A Welsh Wordscape	54
Well-proportioned Panorama	57
Hills	58
R S Visits the City	60
The Light	62
RNLD TOMOS	64

Greg Hill: R. S. Th.	65
Jeremy Hooker: In the footsteps of No-one	66
Emyr Humphreys: S.L. i R.S. (An Imagined Greeting)	69
Mark Jarman: R. S. Thomas	71
Mike Jenkins: Places You Cannot Go	72
T. H. Jones: Back?	73
Rupert M. Loydell: Even in Darkness	75
Roland Mathias: Sir Gelli to R. S.	76
John Mole: Eh?	78
Twm Morys: R.S.	79
Gareth Neigwl: Gwarchod	82
Gareth Neigwl and Myrddin ap Dafydd: Cywydd	89
Oliver Reynolds: Thomases Two	91
Owen Sheers: Inheritance	92
Daniel Tobin: A Stone in Aberdaron	93
John Tripp: on hearing r. s. thomas	96
Damian Walford Davies: Villanelle: The Hide	98
Jason Walford Davies: Cinio Gydag R. S.	99
John Powell Ward: A Bride in White	105
Harri Webb: The Next Village to Manafon	106
Ianto Rhydderch: Tch Tch	107
Daniel Westover: At Porth Neigwl	108
Rowan Williams: Deathship	110
John Wood: Two Poems Inspired by M. E. Eldridge	111
Contributors	114
Acknowledgements	121

Foreword

Gareth Neigwl

RS, some would say, courted publicity. To others, he was a stern unsmiling character who kept people at bay. I have heard and read these things, and many other things about him for that matter, but much of this material portrays a slightly different man from the one I knew. Perhaps I have some sort of advantage over many eager to provide the flesh and bones of his character. My wife's roots were cultivated in the soil of Dyffryn Banwy in Maldwyn, not far from Manafon, and he knew her family long before I met her. During those days at Manafon, she recalls tales of RS going on his weekly visits to the Reverend H. D. Owen, then Independent minister near Llanfair Caereinion, to learn Welsh. He would also call to see her father, one of his contemporaries at Bangor University; the young RS passionately in pursuit of conversational practice in his quest to master the language of his country.

'One must take the man as one finds him', according to the old word, and in Porth Neigwl both he and Elsi melted into the rural community, living unassumingly amongst us. RS involved himself with many things conducive to the survival of our way of life, ranging from *Llanw Llŷn*, a Welsh-language community newspaper voluntarily produced monthly, to Cyfeillion Llŷn, a group involved with ensuring the survival of the indigenous culture and natural habitat of this beautiful peninsula. Even when he attracted the wrath of the English press for refusing to condemn the holiday home arson campaign of the 1980s, neither he nor his neighbours were too bothered. We all knew that if the

English language was being threatened with extinction by external pressures, and he had spoken out in defence, the same press would have made him a hero!

As a neighbour, he was kind and considerate. He could also be serious, sometimes stern. He could be humorous, thriving on a tongue-in-cheek comment. He was also vulnerable. I remember him telling me, during one of his first winters at Sarn, that he was *'dan y felan'* (low in spirit). Daylight faded at around half past three as shadows from trees at Plas yn Rhiw, overhanging his cottage, served to emphasise *'y dyddiau duon bach'* (the short, dark days of November and December). He obviously missed the light reflecting off the sea at Aberdaron. He was in a similar state of mind when he called at my home one summer evening.

'Not much wind in your sails, RS?'

The reason? 'People! People calling, knocking my door, expecting me to answer! People enquiring whether they are at the poet's cottage. After all, I have chalked plainly on the upper half of the door *Cartref R. S. Thomas*. (R. S. Thomas' home). What on earth is the matter with them? Can't they read? They think they have this divine right to pester me! What is there to find out about a poet? The poet is his poetry. Everything else about him is gossip and trivia!'

'But RS bach, without the gossip and trivia there would be no man, and without the man, there would be no poet,' was my response.

On another occasion it was his mortality. 'I am growing old you know, not as agile as I used to be'.

My response was again rather light-hearted. 'Good heavens, it's all in your mind. You are forever out walking, a pair of binoculars around your neck in pursuit of your bird watching. You look very fit to me'.

'Hm', he responded, quoting Mark Twain, 'age is mind

over matter. If you don't mind it doesn't matter'.

My children were frequent recipients of his kindness. Sometimes RS the baker would arrive with a tin of his currant cup cakes. Every autumn he would arrive with home-grown figs. They were always presented on a plate that Elsi had decorated with a fig leaf. Another time it would be home-made jam, usually blackberry. He was an avid picker of the fruit, spending many an afternoon donned in a long, black PVC-type coat, half-hidden in the hedgerows. This is how it transpired during one of these afternoons circa 1979, according to RS. 'I was busy, very busy filling my pitcher, when I heard a vehicle stop. Hm, another Englishman in need of directions, and expecting me to provide them in English! Why should I have to speak English, I thought, and decided to carry on blackberrying. I heard the car door open, and sensed the driver walking in my direction. Subsequently he touched my elbow, enquiring if my hearing was deteriorating. Do you know who it was? A dear friend from my time at Eglwys Fach paying me a visit. I had not considered that possibility'.

Many a time while he sat in our kitchen, Tomi Puw, our cat, would meander back and forth, rubbing against his trouser legs, as cats do. According to RS, 'Tomi knows full well that I am so fond of birds and thoroughly dislike cats. This is why he insists on rubbing against my trousers like this!'

I once asked him if he'd ever attempted to write poetry in Welsh. This was during a conversation about a poem by Aneirin, a poet who flourished in the sixth century. It describes a ferocious battle at a place called Catraeth, which is present day Catterick in North Yorkshire. He replied negatively, adding that in his opinion, 'One could not compose poetry of value except in one's mother tongue'.

His time here came to an end in the Spring of 1994. RS called to say that he and Betty, who in due course would become his second wife, were moving to Llanfair-yng-Nghornwy, a village not far from Caergybi, where he grew up. She had tripped on the uneven cobbled path at Sarn, and according to RS, her daughter was totally opposed to her staying in such a dangerous place. The smile playing his lips made me think that Betty's daughter had not been so pedantic. But this was RS, a boy in love again, his eyes beaming towards Llanfair-yng-Nghornwy, and a house looking out over Wylfa nuclear power station. 'Full circle, back to my roots', as he put it. I remember spending two successive Christmas eves, 1994 and 1995, with them at their new abode. But it wasn't the old RS. *He* still roamed Mynydd Anelog, the shores of Porth Neigwl, or the trees near Rhydbengan, binoculars around his neck. When we occasionally met during his last couple of years, he left me with the feeling that he regretted leaving Llŷn. He never mentioned it in so many words, but I definitely had that impression.

It is over twenty-one years since Elsi passed away, and nearly nineteen years since RS left Neigwl. I often find myself listening to the tide, a yearning in the whisper of the waves. Such fond memories.

Although his ashes are buried at Porthmadog, the words added on Elsi's stone at Llanfaelrhys are forever appropriate. '*Mewn ysbryd, R. S. Thomas*' (In spirit, R. S. Thomas).

Gareth Neigwl
Porth Neigwl
December 2012

Introduction

'Let it be understood poets / Are dangerous ...'

Thus Emyr Humphreys begins his poem 'S.L. i R.S. (An Imagined Greeting)', in which Saunders Lewis, the S.L. of the title and the most acclaimed and controversial dramatist and critic of modern Wales, speaks to R. S. Thomas, the most acclaimed and controversial poet of modern Wales. In Humphreys' poem, poets are 'lyric terrorists' who detonate 'supernovae ... in a universe of sleeping hearts'. Indeed Thomas' career (like Lewis') was defined by the urge to disturb sleeping hearts – to 'thrust / before congregations hymns / They would prefer not to hear'. It is no wonder that this famously uncompromising and challenging poet has provoked a myriad of poetic responses over the last half century in literary journals, anthologies, poetry collections, and on the Web, primarily in Wales but in other countries as well. Just as Welsh poets between the 1930s and the 1960s necessarily confronted the influence of Dylan Thomas' life and work, poets publishing from the 1960s to the present have had to confront R. S. Thomas' status as the preeminent poet of twentieth-century Wales – a designation not universally commended but spiritedly contested, as a number of the poems collected here demonstrate. This anthology, published on the centenary of his birth in 1913, celebrates the range, depth, and complexity of responses in poetry to Thomas' life and work. I know of no other modern poet who has drawn this level of sustained poetic engagement from contemporaries, due in large measure to the significant role poetry has played – and continues to play – in Welsh culture, and to the ancient and ongoing tradition of Welsh poets addressing their fellow-poets in verse.

Imagined Greetings is not a comprehensive gathering of poems engaging with R. S. Thomas but a selection of those that first and foremost stand on their own *as* poems. The majority of published poems engaging with Thomas are elegies marking his death on 25 September 2000. Many are by established Welsh poets formally mourning a major literary and cultural loss. Tony Conran's 'The Great R. S. is Gone' weaves into its fabric Thomas' distinctive subjects along with touchstone words and phrases: 'the incurious stars', the Machine, the Reservoir, 'the bright field', 'peasants [who] gob at the fire'. Other accomplished elegies include Ruth Bidgood's 'Bereft', Gillian Clarke's 'RS', Menna Elfyn's 'Emyn i Gymro', Twm Morys' 'R. S.', Jeremy Hooker's 'In the footsteps of No-One', and Rowan Williams' 'Deathship'.

The poems in *Imagined Greetings* address not only the poet's death but also his long and immensely productive life. The relationships of authors to R. S. Thomas range from those who knew the man very well over many decades to those who knew him only through his poems. For responses to Thomas the man, the Welsh-language poems provide the most intimate portraits, notably Gareth Neigwl's 'Gwarchod' ('Guarding'), which approaches Thomas as a neighbour in Porth Neigwl on the Llŷn. Myrddin ap Dafydd's 'Awyren uwch angladd R.S.' ('Plane over R. S.'s Funeral') associates Thomas – who learned to speak Welsh as an adult – with Welsh Wales and a shared culture: at the poet's funeral, birds arrive (like R. S.'s poems) 'I loywi .../Un llafn o bladur ein llên' ('whetting a blade of our culture' – Myrddin ap Dafydd's translation). Jason Walford Davies' 'Cinio gyda R. S.' ('Lunch with R. S.') begins with the personally observed and delightfully jarring note that this astringent critic of modern machine culture was a speedy driver ('Nodyn: Yr oedd R. S. Thomas yn yrrwr arbennig o gyflym'). In 'R.S.', Twm Morys thoroughly rejects caricatures of the poet in the popular press as unwelcoming and unloving, asserting the opposite:

> Carai ei wraig, carai win,
> Carai'r ifanc, a'r rafin,
> A charai holl drwch yr iaith,
> Ei hofarôls, a'i hafiaith…

('He loved his wife, he loved wine, he loved the young, and the high-spirited, and he loved the language through-and-through, in its overalls and its mirth …' – Twm Morys' translation.)

My own experience of Thomas contradicts the conventional portrayal of a grumpy recluse: when I met him at a Gregynog Hall conference in 1998, he was wryly funny, pleased to respond to questions about his poetry, and (with my background in mind) forthcoming with opinions about contemporary American poetry. John Wood's 'Two Poems Inspired by M. E. Eldridge', written about a 1981 visit to Thomas' cottage in Porth Neigwl, provides a striking instance of Thomas' forcefully expressed opinions about contemporary poetry: he threw a copy of a new collection by John Ashbury 'hard to the floor' because there's 'not a poem in it'.

* * *

While the majority of poems responding to R. S. Thomas and his work appeared subsequent to his death, a number were published during the poet's lifetime. Some respond by establishing a dialogue with Thomas' original poems: Roland Mathias' 'Sir Gelli to R. S.' speaks to Thomas' poem 'Sir Gelli Meurig'; Emyr Humphreys' 'S.L. i R.S. (An Imagined Greeting)' engages with Thomas' poem 'Saunders Lewis'. Some poets use Thomas originals as launching pads for poems treating related subjects, as with Brian Aspden's 'Travelers in the Dream Trade', which 'remembers' Thomas' 'Monet – The Bas-Bréau Road', and Owen Sheers' 'Inheritance', which originates in Thomas' 'Gifts'. And there are poems drawn from interactions with Thomas or from one of the biographies written about him, including Jane Blank's 'R. S. in Eglwys Fach', John Powell Ward's 'A Bride in White', and Mark Jarman's 'R. S. Thomas'. American responses to Thomas' life and work comprise a significant sub-set of poets in *Imagined Greetings*, including William V. Davis, Jon Dressel, Mark Jarman, Daniel Tobin, Daniel Westover, and John Wood.

Given Thomas' prominence within Wales and abroad, it is not surprising that many poems contest or interrogate his life, political and cultural opinions, public persona, and most iconic poems, beginning with the earliest, T. H. Jones' 1964 'Back?'[1] In 'Well-Proportioned Panorama', Peter Finch dissects 'Welsh Landscape', a famous and controversial early Thomas poem, by sending the text back and forth between 'two translation engines', as Finch explains in an interview: 'On each journey randomness would intervene and the text would move progressively further and further from its origin'.[2] The translation process applies a layer of irony to the elevated tone of 'Welsh Landscape', preserving touchstone words and phrases such as 'the machine' and 'peasants' but distorting, exaggerating, or rendering incomprehensible Thomas' familiar early style and subjects, generating a parody that is simultaneously a critique. Finch's 'Well-Proportioned Panorama', Harri Webb's 'Ianto Rhydderch: Tch Tch', and John Mole's 'Eh?' are all parodies that challenge Thomas at the level of style and subject while interrogating the means by which a poet's style gains currency and influence.

Rather than invoking Thomas' distinctive style, John Tripp's 'on hearing r. s. thomas' offers an opposing poetic method, drawing from American Beat-era poetics, with a self-revelatory persona and unconventional punctuation and typography. Here, Thomas – described while giving a poetry reading – is the 'grey peninsula priest / in off-peg grey suit / limp red tie / spare'. Tripp wonders 'how much of that / dislocated prayer / god's torture in public / was true?' If Thomas' poems are in fact 'true', then Tripp's opposing style and poetics might well be 'false', casting into question Tripp's authority as a poet, his understanding of poetry, even his Welsh identity. In direct contrast to Greg Hill's 'R. S. Th.', which defends Thomas from his critics, reproducing the poet's style as an *homage*, Tripp's conversational voice and confessionalist-cum-beat-poet persona contest Thomas' poetry at the level of self-presentation, opposing Thomas' austere and distancing persona with Tripp's embracing and intimate alternative. In exposing cultural and literary divides operating in Wales during the 1970s, Tripp articulates what must have been a widespread perplexed and resentful reaction within Wales to Thomas' accelerating reputation – launched by established English literary powerbrokers (primarily John Betjemin and Al Alvarez) and consolidated by the bestowing of English literary honors, such as the Royal Society of Literature's W. H. Heinemann Award and the Queen's Gold Medal for Poetry. Indeed, the poems in *Imagined Greetings* are as much about the authors and their own backgrounds – and particular stances on aesthetics, culture, religious belief, and politics – as they are about their immediate subject.

Two poets – Peter Finch and Jon Dressel – contribute the greatest number of poems to this anthology. Finch's engagement with Thomas spans four decades, from 'A Welsh Wordscape', published in 1971, to the ongoing 'R. S. Thomas Information' project', available on Finch's website[3] – and is certainly the most sustained response of any poet. The poems by Welsh-American Jon Dressel featuring his character Dai (or in the case of 'Cân Rhyfelwr' – 'Warrior's Song' – an unnamed younger version of Dai) are in part a complex multi-layered dialogue with Thomas' Iago Prytherch poems, interweaving homage, parody, and critique from a trans-Atlantic perspective.

* * *

While this collection offers a rich diversity of style, subject, and attitude – from the most intimate to the overtly hostile – readers will also discover common threads. One significant thread is that of *struggle* – struggle for and against Thomas' poetics and politics; struggle to come to terms with the poet's absence from the literary scene in Wales; and a struggle to articulate exactly what Thomas' impact has been on Welsh culture and literature. Readers have also struggled with Thomas' subtle and insistent explorations of faith and religious belief in an era when such subjects are seldom addressed in English-language poetry. 'Who is this man / who proclaims himself no-one?' Jeremy Hooker asks in his poem 'In the footsteps of No-one'.[4] There are at least as many answers to Hooker's question as there are poems in this anthology – and the disparate understandings of and relationships to Thomas and his work are suggested by varied representations of the poet's name in poem titles: 'R. S.', 'RS', 'R.S.', 'R.S. Thomas', 'r. s. thomas', 'RNLD TOMOS' and 'R. S. Th'. For some in Wales, Thomas' death would bring relief: 'a hair shirt / Safely defrocked, and the white body it teased / Irrationally red and shameful, now shan't hurt' (from Tony Conran's 'The Great R. S. is Gone'). And yet Thomas would simultaneously remain (again in Conran's words), 'Our Reverend' – intimately and inescapably possessed by the national culture of Wales.

Readers of Thomas' poetry will not be surprised to find a continuous presence of birds in the poems of *Imagined Greetings*, reflecting Thomas' lifelong dedication to birding. The stork, ostrich, eagle, curlew, blue tit, goatsucker, nighthawk, owl, red kite and others make appearances as real creatures, images, and metaphors. In her poem 'Titw Tomos' Menna Elfyn describes Thomas as 'yn caru pob curiad / o'r adain mewn ffurfafen', or 'loving every beat of a wing / that's in the sky' in Elin ap Hywel's translation. In 'S.L. i R.S.' Emyr Humphreys ironically compares Thomas to an ostrich before invoking the tale of the eagle from the Fourth Branch of *The Mabinogi*, to assert the potentially transformative role the Welsh poet may claim:

> A poet can become a bird
> So that intelligent pigs can feed
> On the flesh as it drops
> from the burning branches.

Five decades of poetic engagement with Thomas' life and work has resulted in a wide-ranging and profound body of work that, to quote Walt Whitman in a different context, 'contain[s] multitudes'. Thomas the poet was indeed 'dangerous', a 'lyric terrorist' as Emyr Humphreys asserts poets must be if they are to fully serve their vocation. He was also beloved, un-loved, admired, envied, resented, imitated, scorned, and defended. Nearly every human emotion and attitude seems at some point to have been attached to the man or his work. Still, the full extent of the impact of this iconic and yet entirely human poet on poetry in Welsh and in English will not be known for decades to come:

> Ah, but a rare bird is
> rare. It is when one is not looking,
> at times when one is not there
> that it comes.
>
> R. S. Thomas, 'Sea-watching'

David Lloyd
Le Moyne College
Syracuse, NY
USA
December 2012

---

[1] Dated in *The Complete Poems of T. H. Jones* (Gomer Press, Llandysul, UK: 1977): 439. My thanks to Dr. Katie Gramich, who brought this poem to my attention.
[2] Ian Davidson and Zoe Skoulding, 'Peter Finch Interview: http://www.argotistonline.co.uk/Finch%20interview.htm
[3] Its length precludes publication here. See http://www.peterfinch.co.uk.
[4] 'No-One' is the English title for Thomas' autobiography 'Neb', in *Autobiographies*, trans. Jason Walford Davies (London: Dent, 1997).

Dannie Abse

Is Creation a Destructive Force?

(A question for R.S. Thomas on his 80th birthday)

In the studio where he suddenly died,
on the easel still, pale Ramon's last canvas,
entrancing, unfinished, and of course unsigned.

Afflicted self-portrait. Ramon crouches before
a half-open door – there's dark darkness behind
and, just visible, a stark foot's advancing.

Myrddin ap Dafydd

Awyren uwch angladd R.S.

Down si hei lwli o'r lôn
A diosg hetiau duon
I adrodd am drai Deudraeth
Uwch coed melyn un a aeth.
Oer a llipa yw'r llepian
Di-gerdd, di-emyn, di-gân:
Mae'n aeafau Manafon
Ar y byw; mae'n rhewi i'r bôn
Heb un ffegyn o goffâd
Neu fanadl o ddyfyniad.

Ond dros lli'r weddi, daw rheg
Tonnau o hen ddiwtoneg
Un ryfeles o'r Fali
A phoer lond ei ffarwel hi.

Ac yna, drwy'r ddôr gynnes
Daw rhai o adar R.S.
I loywi drwy ddail ywen
Un llafn o bladur ein llên.

Like a Lullaby

Like a lullaby, we cross the lane and shake our funeral hats, whispering about the lost land under the autumn leaves of a lost man. The ebb-waters are cold and timid without a verse, a hymn or a song. It's a Manafon winter on those of us who are left; bleak without a word of remembrance or a line of his spring bloom.

Suddenly the Teutonic swear of a low-flying fighter jet tears across the flow of a prayer, spitting on the embrace of memory. It is then that a few of RS's favourite characters sing their arrival at the sunlit porch, whetting a blade of our culture through the shadows of the yews.

(translation by Myrddin ap Dafydd)

Roy Ashwell

R.S. Writes His Biography in a New Tongue

Thomas in his final curacy
and caring now for his soul's cure only
set his English to the door
and strove in Welsh to make good his end,
confessed himself thrice
to purge the harsh years from his life,
troubled shepherd, questioning priest,
and took the inward road to where,
before all gospels start,
reluctant god paused for him at last
and spoke the solitary word,
begin.

Bryan Aspden

Travellers In The Dream Trade

Who bothers where this road goes?
(R. S. Thomas: 'Monet – The Bas-Bréau Road')

Silent; not for getting anywhere? No,
they're for going full pelt on, nose bent
by Northern cobbles, guzzling miles
through the day's gruel, hunts and time trials.

In the Café Mec waiting for rain to stop,
curtained by fog, the runny window frames
a dumbshow of poets, cyclists, painters –
culture's hardmen pickled in Bock.

One gap and they're knocking back
Beauce wheatfields, villages sweet as a bird's throat.
Stage wins, an express love for summer's country
fill their heads, afloat on the blond stream,

these travellers in the dream trade who'd pay out
heart's gold for a yellow shirt, and sport
badges of old blood. 'Give it all you've got;
when you die, you die.' Wheels argue the toss.

Spokes and arms, a sorry ditchful mourns
as massed bands of knees go by. Then the slow uphill ballet
till sober among sheepbells and drystone trickles
they taste the rare chateau-bottled air.

The road falls steep as water. They take the plunge.
Tucked under shirts in the downhill chill,
Paris Soir, Bild, de Volkskrant prattle,
shooting the asphalt rapids. Through tar ripple

where Camargue heat waves the leaders on
nothing's in view but the road and riders.
Pied and stripy they are the scenery,
watching who's gone too far, who's come unstuck

In a rear wheel waltz clutching the hedge
to their bosom; weeping alone on the road
or perched by the roadside, pink as a flamingo.
A loose tuft wavers till the broom car sweeps it up.

Was the winning post a dead end?
Better not finish the race whose prize
is to stop riding? Trees like men waiting
give this inkling in the cold: growth is to come.

White-flagged, the square surrenders to winter.
Cars are overtaken by the bread queue.
In the café's din sore heads thicken the stew.
It's 19 – – The Winter Circus begins.

Ruth Bidgood

Bereft

(in memory of R. S. Thomas)

Now is the time
of the dark house,
the empty shore.
Now the argument
is between us, unaided,
and the great Absence.
We have lost the one
who had words to catch
a wordless resonance.
We have lost his sharp cuts,
his logic's elegance.
He is not to be found
by black hearth, bare altar.
Vainly we search for him
in the processions
of sea-creatures at their mass,
and in the sky-wide whirr
of the migrations.
Bereft, we cling
to his image of mercy
in crevices of rock,
to the hope of finding,
as he did one day, the meaning
of a sombre landscape
in a single sunlit field.

Jane Blank

R. S. Thomas in Eglwys Fach

Without the proper ways a man came to Fferm y Cysgod.
A minister of the church, but these were chapel people.
He was tall, they were small.
He sat, long legs crossed loosely (his good shoes shone)
and spoke to her.
All the time her two girls stood by the window, watching
this spider with a voice like their father's singing
one red, one dark, the way the Welsh are.

Their mother lay as a grey stone.
He worked with his words but it was
not even as if raindrops fell slowly to dissolve that stone.

for she was young
and a woman and he was not the Doctor to be in
her bedroom with his handsome face.

He left then, through the house
past the silent baby whose bottle
curdled by a small fire.

Alone, words drove his feet;
only words for the woman whose depression
had such weight she could not stand,
so many words
that span the black mass of the mountain out of focus,
an ant's nest of words that writhed under the mockery
of the matchless stars;
past his dark church
through the night,

faster and faster while they demanded to be held,
suspended in the pattern on a page

until he reached the house
sat before the small window
took his pen and
stilled those beating wings.

Gillian Clarke

RS

His death
on the midnight news.
Suddenly colder.

Gold September's driven off
by something afoot
in the south-west approaches.

God's breathing in space out there
misting the heave of the seas
dark and empty tonight,

except for the one frail coracle
borne out to sea,
burning.

Tony Conran

The Great R.S. is Gone

Our Reverend's dead, and our discomfort eased.
    The stubborn irritant's like a hair shirt
Safely defrocked, and the white body it teased
    Irrationally red and shameful, now shan't hurt.

Peasants, if any are left, can walk the hill,
    Slither to Saturday towns, gob at the fire,
Their minds' vacancy unremarked on still,
    Left to incurious stars and the black mire.

God's sparring partner's finally checkmate.
    Machine and Reservoir stare us in the eye.
Petrol's run out, and our Cynddylan's late
    On that damned tractor in a gap of sky.

The bright field is in shadow. The rarity
He watched in vain for, crowds the silken sea.

John Davies

R.S. Thomas

1. Some comfortable harbour, say,
   tugs a boat like its own
   from the sea. Moored,
   strangeness brings the storm.

   Nights flicker.
   And there is the manse's attic
   blown, one curtain,
   a lighthouse marvelling
   at the bouncing moon.

2. We stood accused
   of reading him. Wrong
   language, place, wrong century.
   Though his shadows from the fields
   match ours, he made his own world,
   lashed it for not surviving.
   Which way forward but back?
   His territory only boulders
   gripped like knuckles.
   It was shrinking always.
   Rage kept him reinforced –
   until, falling short
   of himself, in the light
   that language cannot span,
   he saw a rimless world
   extend the gifted heart's idea
   of self, which is poetry.

3. Wind in the throes of turning
   sighs that we have no centre.
   He is our capital of echoes.

   Places we find ourselves
   not often, store voices far
   from aerials turned to base –

   one voice can set the whole
   wood calling. And one wood asks
   how earth and the planets

   hang together, trees lit
   by a bright field,
   mild locals in eternity.

   He reaped necessities:
   dreams, with slant light
   through our crowded sleep.

   Waking, our harvest beyond
   pylons skewering the hills,
   was new land opened.

William Virgil Davis

First Light

(for R. S. Thomas in memory)

I climb the steep stone
steps, glassy with cold,
to enter the empty church.
Faint light swords through
the upper dark. No wind
murmurs. No candles burn.
No God waits there nor wakes.

Last night, quite abruptly,
it began to rain. And then,
before morning, the rain
turned slowly to snow. And
then again, before first
light, almost imperceptibly,
the snow turned back to rain.

The Island

(after R. S. Thomas)

A great gust of wind blew in
from the sea and the small
island shook. He looked
down, passing his hand
over the ocean and the land,
and watched as the trees
bent back upright and the wind
died down. He smiled as
the few creatures peered
out from their hiding places
and began to move about,
watching over their shoulders.

When they started to sing
and dance, he sent a sharp
crack of thunder and a flash
of lightening that burst
and burned over the top
of the highest hill, where the
ceremonies were always held.
The creatures ran and hid
again and his echoing laughter
rolled over the roiled waters
and disappeared in distance.

Jon Dressel

Dai, Live

Prytherch is dead. We have no right
to doubt it, let alone dispute. We must
contend with men we have in sight,

like Dai here, who is clean
as dirt. The rumor in the pub
is that he hasn't been seen

out of that ripening outfit
since the Investiture. It may
be a form of protest, though it

seems more likely, ten pints down,
he's just too whipped to shuck that
wind-grey coat, every button gone,

peel those frazzling sweaters, rife with him
and earth, let those grime-stiff trousers
fall, or try to fall, before things dim.

Too whipped, perhaps, to kick those mud-
brindled boots to a corner, or toss
that crust of a cap to a bed-

post, if he has one. No farmer, Dai,
he digs around the village, roads,
sewers, God knows what, digs all day,

digs everywhere, turns up pints,
grubs of coins for the slots, studies men
who commute to Carmarthen, nods, squints,

grunts a little rugby, weathers at his end
of the bar like a cromlech, drones
like the surf when those with more voice bend

the last elbow in hymn, leaves alone
with a guttural wave, boulders into night,
a man-shape hulking like an age of stone,

that knows no women, but lives with what it knows,
hard as breath, or a December rose.

Note to a Character

Dai i was hoping to write my traditional
return to wales poem featuring you since
you do have this uncanny knack for being
the first person i see in the village but
there's been a lot of comment about your
kind lately and how you're sort of a crea-
ture of pink romantic blinders or if not
quite that certainly an edifice construct-
ed out of all proportion to its base or if
not quite that at least the last of a species
about which nothing much can be said but that
anyway i was walking the meadow path to the
pub still feeling missouri like lead in my
jet lag when I saw this gaunt black dog half
wolfhound half god knows what coming on it was
strange and fierce and flashing tongue
and fang for a moment i thought i was in
an old sherlock holmes movie there's fantasia
for you boyo but then i saw you close behind
risen from dirt as ever stubbling through
the drouth-scythed field a limp black rabbit
or something in your hand it was dead of course
by dog or sling or snare or whatever i haven't
talked to you since it doesn't matter i just
waved and passed by resolute as odysseus
fast to my mast of resistance to metaphor
the pub was mobbed i nursed a pint of mild
made off about ten took my time walking home
brewed a cup of bovril read a little betjeman
watched the tv closedown had a pee and went to bed.

Dai on Holiday

Dai, you startled me, I had been away
six months, back to Missouri, and when
I came into the pub there you were,
in a tweed jacket looking like a thing
exhumed, a white shirt soiled as Job's
boiled sheet, trousers from a dead Sunday
suit, shapeless, held, barely, by a thick
belt gathering without the help of loops,
and shoes, mud-bronzed, in place of boots;
a quantum change, but of the village,
even so; it was that thing on your head,
that cockeyed halo of a crumpled blue
beret, that did me in; it was not
some soldiered surplus from the market,
but Basque, or French, apache, rakish, wise,
reeking of bistros, women's necks, and wine;
and you'd shaved; you face was strangely
white; you'd gashed, and stanched, your chin; still,
the truth was there, fifty-nine years of weather,
forty-three of ale, the man-virgin eyes,
alien, fierce, intact, beneath the brow's mute
crease on crease; they fixed on me; you nodded,
silently smiled, parting your lips till the dreg
of your fag, a finger-stub of ash, hung,
about to flower, from your toothless upper
gum; I stood beside you, dumb; 'he's on
holiday,' whispered someone later, in a crowd.

Dai Communicates

Dai it's uncanny, again you were the first
of all the village men I saw in the pub
when we came back from Missouri; a year
it had been, you were on your way out,
we almost collided; the glint of recognition
was duller in your eye, I said hello,
you nodded, grunted past and went; you were
full of mild and in need of a crust or
whatever it is you scavenge for supper
(some joke of mice, but there is no cat
nor owl in you, just horse, and stone); two nights
later, showing the publican and two clean
friends some photos of a tavern on a
corner in Saint Louis I felt the need
to bring you in somehow, you for whom
Swansea is the end of the world, wedged silent
against the wall at the end of the bar;
I took the pictures down, went through the stack,
pointing out friends, American beer signs,
explaining all in my best midwestern English;
you looked bewildered, but you smiled, around
your fag; da iawn, da iawn da iawn, you said.

Dim Cyffesu

Lowell or Plath, Anne Sexton, the lot,
would not be comfortable here,
in the country pub at noon at the end

of a river; no Harvard-fine catharses
to be had round here, where guilt and sin
and failure are both opaque and transparent,

like the clear glass windows of the Baptist chapel,
blazing coldly in October sun; ale and rugby here,
and coal-smoke in the air; the decline of Brahmin

families, the failure of daddies, the inadequacies
of relationships, marital or otherwise,
find no articulator in snaggle-tooth Dai,

celibate as dust for sixty years; divorce
and lost daughters, the suicidal urge,
surface through no eye of taut lean Ioan

with the thickening wife, who dreams whatever
dreams he has and tips his pint in silence;
here, California does not exist, and there

are no programs in group sensitivity;
rain takes all the blame for the mildew
here, where more children than not just

grow up and stay put; at a skunk hour here,
they simply go to bed; this is the dead end
of Wales, unconfessed, alive, still saved.

Cân Rhyfelwr

A tough lot. You, the whole family.
After ten o'clock, I steer clear
of you in the pub. You'd just as

soon have a punch-up as a short
at closing. I used to chalk it
just to your frustrations, your

bankruptcies, your dogged little
handyman enterprises that never
quite come off. Your daughters

leave school early and foal. Your
sons are not clever but are good
with their hands. Your wife pumps

petrol. Her arms are thick as yours.
The woodwork on your council house
goes blistered and bare. You work

elsewhere. They say you were
fierce at rugby once. Monoglot
English from birth, you were all

I despaired of in the figure of Wales.
You were the gwerin, beaten thin
at last, sullen, unremembering, nothing

but a bloke. Then I saw you this morning,
in a field with a standing stone
at the edge of the village. You had

a red horse, in the early sun,
and you raced it round and round
you in what seemed a great clean circle

of the flesh made blaze, its head high,
your eyes raised, intent, as though
you held it by your gaze more than

the long thin lead. You hardly moved.
You turned like stone. It was
just work, yet something more essential

than the stress of small contracting
put the pressure on your blood.
You wheeled the taut red horse like fire,

that whole half hour. It was your work,
yet tired land rose, the land had force,
the clean horse came, the sunned stone sang.

Menna Elfyn

Y Bardd Di-flewyn

Golchi'r byd yn lân bob bore
yw swydd afrwydd y bardd.

'Gwrych sy gennyf,' meddai wrthyf.
Ac heb feddu offer eillio na chysur balm

Allan â ni i'r ddinas fawr, rhyw ddau alltud
ar driwant, cerdded y palmant a'r Sul yn ddi-salm.

Yr hirdrwch yn ei boeni'n fawr. Ac eto?
'Onid gweddus,' meddwn, 'yw gwrych a dardd

ar ên un sy'n codi gwrychyn?' A chil-
wenu a wnest wrth i bob man droi'n ddi-lafn.

A dychwelasom yn waglaw. Ddoe ddiwethaf
fe gofiais yr hyn yr ofnais ei ddweud yn blaen.

O, fel y gallet fod wedi dal yn dy ysgrifbin.
Onid min oedd iddo, a rasel, i wella'r graen

gan frathu'n glós pob wyneb; llyfnu bochau'n glir
o bob gwrychiau? Onid plannu llafn

a chael y genedl hon yn gymen wnest? O drwch blewyn.
Crafu'n agos i'r wythïen las nes iasu'n gwedd.

A chlywed anadl drom arnom – cyn pereiddio grudd.
Dau beth sy'n groes i'r graen yw eillio ac eli

fel y ddeuddyn ynot. Ar wrych wrth chwilio'n sylwedd
ond â llaw lonydd sad, at sofl enaid, hyd y diwedd.

The Poet

To wash the world new every morning,
that's the poet's work.

'I have a hedge,' he told me.
And no razor. No aftershave.

Off we went into the city, two exiles
bunking off, walking the psalmless Sunday streets.

His mind was on stubble. Yet,
'Surely it's right,' I said, 'that prickles grow

On the chin of a man who's a thorn in our side?'
You half smiled, and everywhere bladeless.

We returned empty-handed. Just yesterday
I remembered what I wanted to say:

You could pick up your pen,
razor-sharp, and sleek skin with it,

shave every cheek, smooth every face
of wrinkles. Haven't you, bit by bit,

close-shaved the nation within a hair's breadth,
scraped close to the vein till the skin gasped

and we felt the blade's breath before the balm?
Two things at odds, the balm and the blade,

like the men in you, one needling our minds,
The other with a still steady hand on our souls, in the end.

(translation by Gillian Clarke)

Cusan Hances

Mae cerdd o'i chyfieithu fel cusan drwy hances.
R.S. Thomas

Anwes yn y gwyll?
Rhyw bobl lywaeth oeddem

yn cwato'r gusan ddoe.
Ond heddiw, ffordd yw i gyfarch

ac ar y sgrin fach, gwelwn
arweinwyr y byd yn trafod,

hulio hedd ac anwes las;
ambell un bwbach. A'r delyneg

o'i throsi nid yw ond cusan
drwy gadach poced, medd ein prifardd.

Minnau, sy'n ymaflyd cerdd ar ddalen
gan ddwyn i gôl gariadon-geiriau.

A mynnaf hyn. A fo gerdd bid hances
ac ar fy ngwefus

sws dan len.

Handkerchief Kiss

A poem in translation is like kissing through a handkerchief.
R. S. Thomas

A caress in the dark.
What a tame lot we were,

with our secretive yesterday's kisses.
Today, it's a common greeting,

and we watch on the small screen
world leaders deal peace

with a cold embrace,
or an adder's kiss. The lyric

translated is like kissing
through a hanky, said the bard.

As for me, I hug those poems between pages
that bring back the word-lovers.

Let the poem carry a handkerchief
and leave on my lip

its veiled kiss.

(translation by Gillian Clarke)

Titw Tomos

Fe glywodd cynulleidfa gyfan un titw yn cadw twrw yn ystod Gŵyl dathlu bywyd R.S. Thomas ym Mhortmeirion yn 2002. Ond daeth y titw yno gyntaf, y prynhawn cyn y perfformiad pan oedd y bardd ar ei phen ei hun yn disgwyl y delynores.

Ymarfer ar gyfer gŵyl
nes i sioc y gnoc,
    geincio ffenest;
yn ddi-sgôr yno'n telori
    un titw Tomos bach,
wrth y cware, ac o'r cracie
    galwodd arnaf o'r cyrion.

Plyciodd fel pe mewn plygain,
    dim ond fe a fi
a neb arall,
    dau big mewn unigedd.

Yna, yng nghlyw'r delyn,
    dychwelodd i blycio,
ei adain yn troelli,
    ac i sain tannau, ymunodd
â'r gyngerdd o'i werddon.

Drannoeth,
    daeth glas y pared
yn ôl i weld hen ffrindiau,

wrth i rai sôn amdano,
yn caru pob curiad
o'i ffrwtian mewn ffurfafen.

A phrofwyd y wireb:
adar o'r unlliw – ehedant...

Eithr cofio'r dieithryn
   a wnaf o hyd,
yr Ebrill bach ebilliodd,
   acenion cyn canu

ti a mi,
   lygad at lygad
yn troi'r neuadd wag yn nyth o ddathliad.

The Stranger

A roomful of listeners heard one blue tit making its presence felt during a celebration of R.S. Thomas' life at Portmeirion in 2002. But the blue tit had first arrived the afternoon before the performance, while the poet was awaiting the harpist.

Rehearsing a festival
I hear a small arpeggio of knocks
shocking the window:
warbling there, scoreless,
one tiny blue tit:
through the panes beyond the frame
he calls to me from the margins.

Trilling as if at matins,
just him and me,
no one else,
two solitary beaks.

Then, in the harp's hearing
he came again to draw his thread of song
on fluttering wings,
harmonising the strains of the harpstrings, chambering
the concert from his oasis.

The next day,
the small singer
returned to see old friends.

Just as some spoke of him,
loving every beat of a wing
that's in the sky.

And so the dictum came to pass –
that birds of a feather do flock together.

And yet I remember the stranger,
the small April he caroled,
the grace notes before the song,
you and me,
eye to eye,
turning the empty hall into a nest of jubilation.

(translation by Elin ap Hywel)

Peter Finch

A Welsh Wordscape

1.

To live in Wales,

Is to be mumbled at
by re-incarnations of Dylan Thomas
in numerous diverse disguises.

Is to be mown down
by the same words
at least six times a week.

Is to be bored
by Welsh visionaries
with wild hair and grey suits.

Is to be told
of the incredible agony
of an exile
that can be at most
a day's travel away.

And the sheep, the sheep,
the bloody flea-bitten Welsh sheep,
chased over the same hills
by a thousand poetic phrases
all saying the same things.

To live in Wales
is to love sheep
and to be afraid
of dragons.

2.

A history is being re-lived,
a lost heritage
is being wept after
with sad eyes and dry tears.

A heritage
that spoke beauty to the world
through dirty fingernails
and endless alcoholic mists.

A heritage
that screamed that once,
that exploded that one holy time
and connected Wales
with the whirlpool
of the universe.

A heritage
that ceased communication
upon a death, and nonetheless
tried to go on living.

A heritage
that is taking
a long time to learn
that yesterday cannot be today
and that the world
is fast becoming bored
with language forever
in the same tone of voice.

Look at the Welsh landscape,
look closely,
new voices must rise.
for Wales cannot endlessly remain
chasing sheep into the twilight.

Well-Proportioned Panorama

Alive in Wales is informed
At dusk of an opposite blood
That has been going about as a manufactured savage sky
    product,
Dying our immaculate books.
They all have understood their expenses
It has to be said.
Above the noisy tractor
And the virile bee of the machine.
It is the dissension in the drink that they ache,
Vibrant with acclimatised arrangements.
You can live with peasants
At last in Wales.
There is the linguaphone for example,
Consonants that have the candy
Strange to the ear,
There is the shout in the Gogledd this evening
Similar to owls on the moon,
And a heart shitting in the bushes,
Calming the polyester of the hills.
It has never been the present in Wales,
And the future
Is a racy bodice-ripper stolen from the past,
Fragile with Vernacular
A colon-exhaled nibble mansion
With imposing ghosts
Misunderstood exploits and men
Of infirm person,
Cancelling their traverses,
To widdle on the dictionaries of a polyurethane song.

Hills

Just an ordinary man of the bald Welsh hills,
docking sheep, penning a gap of cloud.
Just a bald man of the ordinary hills,
Welsh sheep gaps, docking pens, cloud shrouds.
Just a man, ordinary, Welsh doctor, pen weaver
cloud gap, sheep sailor, hills.
Just a sharp shard, hill weaver, bald sheep,
pilot pen rider, gap doctor, cloud.
Just a shop, sheer hill weaver, slate,
balder, cock gap, pen and Welsh rider,
Just slate shop, hill balder, cocking,
shop gap. Welsh man, cloud pen.
Just shops, slate, cocks, bald sheep,
Welsh idea, gutteral hills, ordinary cloud.
Just grass gap, bald gap, garp grap,
grap shot sheep slate, gap grap.
garp gap
gop gap
sharp grap shop shap
sheep sugar sha
shower shope sheep
shear shoe slap sap
grasp gap gosp gap
grip gap grasp gap
guest gap grat gap
gwint gap grog gap
growd gap gost gap
gap gap gwin gap
gap gop gwell gap
gap gop gap gap

gap gap gap gap
gap gap gorp gap
gap gap gap gap
gap gap gap gap
gap gap gap gap
gap gap gap gap
gap gap gap
immigrant slate mirth grot gap
bald grass, rock gap, rumble easy,
old gold gap, non-essential waste gap,
rock docker, slow slate gap, empty rocker,
rate payer, wast gap, cloud hater,
grasper balder, pay my money, dead,
trout shout, slate waste, language nobody
uses, bald sounds, sends, no one pens,
fire gap, failed gasps,
dock waste, holiday grey gap,
hounds, homes, plus fours, grip sheep,
four-wheeled Rover: Why not? Soft price,
grown gravel, sais
The problem gaps, ordinary television,
nationalist garbage, insulting ignorance,
shot sheep, invited bald interference,
don't need real sheep where we are,
sheepless, sheepless, Welsh as you are, still,
no gasps, gogs or gaps for us,
no,
point our aerials at the Mendip Hills.

R S Visits The City

This city is now spinning like an exhibition
for cities. Clear and clean. Full of aspiration
and landmark work. Sort of rocks.
Yeats never came to it. Pound
did not. Nor Eliot. What did they want with
barely Welsh drizzle and dirt? RS Thomas did.
A thin faced return in his reverend's suit. Sat
before the snaking queues in the Royal Hotel
siarad am pwrpas, siarad am ysbryd, siarad am iaith,
signing effortlessly his enormous books.

This was the man who'd come to the city
before, years ago, hating it, sitting for thirty minutes
unmoving on stage, not a flicker, even of
his eyes, then slowly undoing his
string-tied bundle of printed matter to read
without interruption or explanation or
even the slightest elevation of the voice
his existential patriotic verse   letting
it swirl into the vortex of our ears. At this 30 year
distance I can't recall
anything of the content only that it
shimmered like dancing motes.
The poet now is himself dust
and the people who knew him faltering. The
celebrated poetry lowering like an aging beast
inside his reprinted books.

In this work are there traces of this place,
where he was born, reluctant, leaving
as fast as he could, do the streets of Cardiff echo?
No, they don't. Do we honour him in this
city as a lost son? Plaque, statue, trail?
No we do not.

Not Welsh enough us, for a man redolent of
revolutionary fire and rural fields.
In Wales cities are alien places.
I had a postcard of him printed, black
and white, shot of a younger man, smiling. I'd destroy
those if I were you, he advised, when I showed
him. Went out the shop door to walk among
Bute's trees in the great park where the air was clean
like it was in Llŷn. And after he'd returned to
his stone cottage where the past burned
but the heating didn't work I put the cards on full display.
Sold the lot.

The Light

R S is striding down the hill through the early morning light. Clear, tight. His jaw stretches like paper. He hasn't shaved perfectly, bristles on the chin are missed. The fields behind him are full of mangles, green top, the soil in overgrown furrows. The hedges stand exactly where they did on the ancient maps. This landscape, his landscape, it doesn't change much.

In his hand he clutches a copy of Peter Meuiller's *Distaff* and the catalogue of book-bound objects showing at the European Centre for Traditional and Regional Culture at Llangollen, Clwyd. Childe Roland's paper book in a bottle, his bindings of torn paper, colours overlaid and rolling like waves, treaties with subject but no content, gestalt whiteness, French and Welsh merging, fel melin, fel ymbarel, fel eli, fel melfa, fel tawel, fel dychwel, What are your plans for the future, my lord, Ham and Jam? There is light in these works; sometimes nothing but. Where else in this northern fastness can you find the word for light repeated so often that it glows. The friction of the signifier, the concrete base of Meuiller's brightness makes sparks in the Welsh air.

Childe Roland to the Dark Tower Came. A poem by Robert Browning published in *Men and Women* (1855). The title comes from a snatch of song recited by Edgar in King Lear. To maintain his practice and his position Browning had resolved to write a poem a day. The Lear song comes from the age of Arthur where Childe Rowland, aided by the instruction of Merlin, makes his way to a castle to rescue his sister who has been carried there by fairies. 'Child Rowland to the dark tower came, / His word was still 'Fie, foh, and fum / I smell the blood of a British man.'

R S hums the snatch, feet in their brogues crushing the earth clod, small dust flurries rise as they pass. The light here has never been good. No depth or range of colour, only grey and green. And the wind blowing. Meuiller in his guise as Childe Roland has adopted these lands. On them he mixes his native Canadian French with the Welsh of the stones. His dissertation was a blank book with a long line running from page one to page three hundred. The line was English, if a line can carry tongue. It sped from where the idea began to where the idea finished. Do ideas finish? R S is unsure.

On the headland facing Ynys Enlli, island of the saints, Bardsey, birds and graves, and holy stones, Roland has assembled a choir. Slowly they sing the Shearwater Oratorio – dit dit dah dit – Roland's Morse code translation of the Manx Shearwater's enigmatic cry. R S wasn't there. The text in his hands is colourless and silent. But on Bardsey, the shearwater's breeding ground, is a cloud of wings, a storm of sound.

R S walks on. You can't rely on things. He knows that. Childe Roland doesn't engage language from the outside. He assembles it from within. R S stuffs the poems inside his coat. Read them again later. Worry about the consequences. Or keep the whole thing a life secret? Behind him the sun's light streams in through the clouds. The paleness banished. Fel cerdd newydd. Nawr.

RNLD TOMOS

(*vcl, hca, some prse*) aka Curtis Langdon. 1913-2000. Gospel. Austerity tradition. Jnd Iago Prytherch Big Band (1959), gog, gap, bwlch, lleyn tân, iaith, mynydd, mangle, adwy – mainly on Hart-Davis race label. Reissue Dent PoBkSoc Special Recommend. Concert at Sherman support Sorley Maclean (*gts, hrt cluching*) sold out. Fire Bomb tour Sain triple CD for D. Walford Davies (*vcl, crtcl harmonium*) new century highspot. A pioneer of dark wounds and internal tensions. In old age bird song and reliable grouch. Stood, was counted, still no change. To live in Wales is to become unassailable. 'An angel-fish' (Clarke). Expect retrospective, marveling and statue.

Greg Hill

R. S. Th.

And they came to him
with their questions, insisting
that he resolve the matter
in their wounds. He told
them of the musings of
the heart's silence, of
a vision he had of
a bird singing in the
serenity of a nation
at peace with itself.

   But strident
voices called in language
that hurt the dignity of
his vision. Again they came
ready now for a confrontation
he could not refuse. He
told them of a nation
that would believe in itself,
of a few that sought to
atone for the indifference
of the rest.

   They erected a floodlit
cross then, and the crows
gathered and croaked in the
gloom about him.

Jeremy Hooker

In the footsteps of No-one

(in memory of R. S. Thomas)

After the closed door, silence.

After the death-fog, emptiness.

After the emptiness, images –

    a shape of words,
we could say,
no bigger than a man's hand,
a cloud, a flock of birds whitening
the March ploughland, blackening
mountains & moorlands & the coasts of Wales,
a mist rising off moist furrows
and the earthen crock of a skull
with its question-mark curl of spirit.

Who is this man
who proclaims himself no-one?
What is his boast?

Old salt, lashed to the father-tree.
Priest on his knees, daring to question
He Who Is Not At Home.
Listener with his ear to the shell
of the church that was Wales,
waiting for a worthy people.

Proud man, nobly infirm, stag
sniffing the air for a rival.
Austere old man, suddenly
skipping like a youth
to the pleasures of his lady.

As for myself, I most remember
a night when his voice refused us
everything but the poem,
which seemed to reach out,
and quavering on the air
came an owl's voice from Powys woods
seeming to answer.

So the images, the cloud,
we might say,
the flock descending
appear to settle, and rise,
as a mist,
leaving moist blades shining.

Afterwards silence
that is a different sound,
the mountains, the moorland, the sea
and the sea-watches
sharper, brighter,
and more the same than we ever knew.

Like a door, we might say,
which the man has opened,
and closed behind him,
leaving it as it always was,
but now too strangely different,
the land of a poet who dared to be human.

Emyr Humphreys

S.L. i R.S. (An Imagined Greeting)

i

Let it be understood poets
Are dangerous: they undermine
The state: they thrust
Before congregations hymns
They would prefer not to sing.

Lyric terrorists disrupt
The best ordered families drive
Favourite sons abroad
In search of nameless ecstasies:
Incite wives and daughters to dance
Before the flickering images
Of unattainable desires ...
Who knows what supernovae
Are denoted in
A universe of sleeping hearts?

ii

You arrived at an unexpected
Hour, emerged
From that Austin Seven
Like an ostrich stretching
His legs as he abandons
The mechanised egg
Eyes washed in primal light
Unused to blinking.

Integrity is a lyric gift
Not a virtue: be warmed for a lifetime
By the hammering of
Unfettered thought
On the anvil of your suffering.

iii

Plato should have consulted
Gwydion Ddewin before
Sending your soul into exile.
Dâr a dyf rhwng dau lyn.
A poet can become a bird
So that intelligent pigs can feed
On the flesh as it drops
from the burning branches.

iv

Er gwaethaf neu oherwydd
Dy gathlau ysblennydd
Ieithwedd anorfod
Gorfoledd a chur
Yn dy galon y Gymraeg a orfu.
Dyna pam y saif cawr
Awenydd a'r oerwynt
Yn ymlid ei gydynnau gwyn
O flaen Llys Barn yn erfyn
Ar y cenedlaethau achub
Ei cham: aderyn y gwyll
Yn ymarfer cân y wawr.

Mark Jarman

R. S. Thomas

To see heaven as a length of seashore
And months of bird watching. To stalk the fells
Like a stork trying to get aloft.
To hear wind and river both as voices
And the word *Christ* like a skin of ice
Crackling under shrill December stars.
One day a week to lift the host
And fortified wine. To have water the rest,
And mutton, cold mutton, mutton stew,
A kipper on Friday, and the desk for poems
And a space of lamplight for the eyes,
Wife and child, like farmers in the combes,
Elsewhere with their own preoccupations,
One God for the drowsy villagers
In the matte black pews, and another,
True God, for the squealing curlew
And the red kite on her found nest.

Mike Jenkins

Places You Cannot Go

'There are places in Wales I don't go' – R. S. Thomas, 'Reservoirs'

There are places in Cymru you cannot go:
Mynydd Epynt and Pendine as foreign
as, to Cuba, is Guantanamo;
places marked off by red flags
the colour of danger not revolution,
with warnings of live ammunition.

These places are rung by high wire,
they are firing ranges:
I think of villages cleared,
of farms left abandoned,
of long beaches and dunes
you can never stride along.

There are fields and there is sand,
occupied in training for wars
from the Falklands to Afghanistan:
if you should pick up those shells
they'd be homes for no-one.

T. H. Jones

Back?

(to R. S. Thomas)

Back is the question
Carried to me on the curlew's wing,
And the strong sides of the salmon.

Should I go back then
To the narrow path, the sheep turds,
And the birded language?

Back to an old, thin bitch
Fawning on my spit, writhing
Her lank belly with memories:

Back to the chapel, and a charade
Of the word of God made by a preacher
Without a tongue:

Back to the ingrowing quarrels,
The family where you have to remember
Who is not speaking to whom:

Back to the shamed memories of Glyn Dwr
And Saunders Lewis's aerodrome
And a match at Swansea?

Of course I'd go back if somebody'd pay me
To live in my own country
Like a bloody Englishman.

But for now, lacking the money,
I must be content with the curlew's cry
And the salmon's taut belly

And the waves, of water and of fern
And words, that beat unendingly
On the rocks of my mind's country.

Rupert M. Loydell

Even in Darkness

(i.m. R.S. Thomas)

Drawing slow lines
(a dark river's silt)

Inherent uncertainty
(echo sound nightmare)

Softly breathe
(safe ground)

Roland Mathias

Sir Gelli to R. S.

Even the worst intelligence must needs ride
Some years to reach me where I am, and hardihood
Bids me to leave yours lie. But that I cannot bear
To be held innocent and frail, a touch
For baubles and fine clothes. As well regret
Your verse for simpering at women. All
That I cherished, all, lay in the head –
The secret webs of a Gladestry morning, sun
Lofting at Wigmore or my other house
Or Llanelwedd, the clustered recusants, puritans
And Essex captains waiting on black-browed
Judgment. There was my Wales in thrall, delivered,
Dumb, to the cause. As for the town, man, London,
When was I there more happentimes than you?
I was at Cadiz, sure enough, with the spoils
To divide for my master, I the black pinnace
Roped to the heaving flagship, provisioner
For the extravagant wars. But London's a place
To pass through for a Welshman, always was. And I
Was no Penfro squirreling with a perch of squill
On the cliff-top, idling it out in a city
Of coneys. I diced and ran with the Devereux, he
And I at Lamphey, boys of the dangerous covert. My
Black looks defended his bright ones. I
Clothed him with darkness, saturnine, setting the meats
For the rout, pricking him dumb men for the sheriffs
Throughout the March, bribing the Assizes' scratch
To a lazy quill for the papists' sake. The magic
Silence there and before my Lord Pembroke's notaries

Was like the spell of Llwyd son of Cil Coed that
   Manawydan
Knew when he came from plying his trade in Lloegr.

I was always a man of silence. Even at Tyburn
When Cuffe, my cumbersome scaffold fellow, pleaded
To make his peace, I cut him short. It
Was no time for wheedling. The Devereux
Was my master, in treason or out. Why demean
His title a moment for such alien grace?
'Set the axe to', I said. Yet you aver
I cried for the baubles. Man, when we meet
I'll bloody you sharply an you'll not declare
Which of us left an innocence in Wales.

John Mole

Eh?

He said: take back your typescripts
creatures. Scribble away
in the silence which is the process
of the absence of the producer
of programmes.
                    Adjust
your sets to the infrequency
of verse, the time's virus
wiping its bacilli
from tangled spools.
                    The lift door
closes with the terminal
susurrus of suspended
operations. It ascends
to that vacancy where you must
shape alone the ultimate
meaning's primal echo
in the studio of the spirit.

Twm Morys

R.S.

Mae'r hen wynt fu gynt o'i go'
Heddiw drwy'r Rhiw yn rhuo,
A sŵn y derw'n y don
A dyrr yn Aberdaron.
Mae hi'n dymor mynd o'ma
Ar holl wenoliaid yr ha'.
Ond mae'r adar yn aros
Ar y graig arw a'r rhos.

Be' welodd yr hac boliog – o Lundain,
    A landiodd mor dalog?
    Nid brenin ar ei riniog,
    Nid dyn trist, a'i Grist ar grog,

Ond dyn gwyllt, fel dewin o'i go'. – Hyll iawn
    Yw'r lluniau ohono:
    R.S. sych yn ei ddrws o,
    Ac R.S. oer ei groeso.

R.S. yn oer ei groeso?
Nid i'r un o'i adar o!
Carai ei wraig, carai win,
Carai'r ifanc, a'r rafin,
A charai holl drwch yr iaith,
Ei hofarôls, a'i hafiaith ...

Bu'r gwaith, a'r bara a'r gwin
Olaf ym Mhentrefelin,
Ac mae'r gwynt drwy Gymru i gyd,

Manafon, a Môn hefyd.
Mae hi'n dymor mynd o'ma
Ar holl wenoliaid yr ha'.
Ond mae'r adar yn aros
Ar y graig arw a'r rhos.
Aros byth, R.S., y bydd
Adar mân dewr y mynydd.

R.S.

That furious wind of long ago is roaring today in Rhiw, and the noise of the oak trees is in the wave that breaks in Aberdaron. It's time to leave for all the swallows of summer. But the birds remain on the rugged rock and the moor.

What did that fat hack from London see when he landed so cockily? Not a king on his doorstep, not a man sad for his crucified Christ, but a wild man, a mad wizard. The pictures of him were ugly: a dry R.S. in his doorway, a cold-welcome R.S.

Cold-welcome R.S.? Not to any of his own birds! He loved his wife, he loved wine, he loved the young and the high-spirited, and he loved the language through-and-through, in its overalls and its mirth...

The final bread and wine was in Pentrefelin, and the wind is blowing all through Wales; in Manafon and Anglesey. But the birds remain on the rugged rock and the moor. They will stay forever, R.S., the brave little birds of the mountain.

(translation by Twm Morys)

Gareth Neigwl

Gwarchod

Hen ddyn a'i wely'n alaw
I olau haul, gwynt a glaw
Welai nos ein cenedl ni,
Eithinog ei charthenni.
Yn ei lais roedd ing ei wlad
Gwae y môr drwy'i gymeriad.

I'w glyw daeth Neigwl a'i don,
A naws iâ yn ei suon;
Y tonnau'n geffylau gwyn,
Ac oriau eu gwehyru'n *
Ei flino, tafla'i wyneb
I'w droi yn ôl i dir Neb.
A'r nos â'i hoerni'n iasol
A'i synau'n wich, oesau'n ôl.

    * * *

Yn ôl y don, fesul dydd
Ei oriawr fu'r Iwerydd
I'w bwnio o'i obennydd.

I wylio hefo'r wylan.
Fel dôi ei lef led y lan,
A'i gilwg tros y geulan!

Taniai fel ymchwydd tonnau,
Tanio a'i wên yn tynhau,
Tanio â'i wyneb tenau.

Yn ei ofn fe'n dwrdiai ni,
Â'i enaid yn ymboeni.
Neu'n wyllt ŵr yn llwyd ei wedd,
Mynych yn ddiamynedd.
Ei dafod, ein dyfodol,
Ei siars hir, erys o'i ôl.

Er geiriau'n rhaeadr gorwyllt,
Yn swyn ei gerdd, rosyn gwyllt,
Erys yn chwa'r rhosmari
Rin ei ardd drwy'n ffroenau ni;
Wrth wiail traeth ei awen
Dyn oedd a'i lygaid yn wên.

* * *

Ar awel hefo'r ewyn y daw o
    Hyd allt a thros dywyn;
    O'i bridd oer daw'r bardd ei hun
Yn fythol i'w hen fwthyn.

Rhy'i amser i aderyn ar y wawr,
    Bri'r wyrth yn y brigyn;
    Hen alaw y Maen Melyn,
A'i holl lais dros harddwch Llŷn.

Ein hiaith, ei obaith o hyd, ei allor,
    Diwylliant ein bywyd,
    A'i lef o rhag cenedl fud,
Cyfoed â'r ifanc hefyd.

Rhy'eto yn eu protest
Loesau'r fron, â'i lais o'r frest,
Y gorchwyl yn lle gorchest.

O garchar ei ymgyrchoedd
Rhy' ddur y bladur mewn bloedd
Â'i haul yn gyffro'r miloedd.

Tra'n magu hyder Erin
I droi y sychau i'r drin,
O'i ofid tros gynefin.

Y mae rhwyd mewn camerâu,
Dau wn mewn rhai cwestiynau;
Ond yn don daw'r dyn o'i dŷ.
Â hyd Neigwl dan wgu!
Yn y gwynt mae'i fyddin gudd,
Eu henwau? Gŵyr y mynydd.

Yn y don mae'r cread oedd,
Ei iaith hyf a'i eithafoedd;
Un hen ŵr i'n cyfiawnhau,
Un wyneb i'r ugeiniau
Tawel, ond si yr heli
O lannau'i nwyf a glywn ni.
Yn rhannu ei her heno,
Cau mur â'r ifanc mae o.

* * *

Seilam eu nos o olau,
A'i foliwm hi fel y mae
O dai'r hwyr, hwylia i'r stryd,
A rhwyfo'r aber hefyd,

Yn sŵn rhai ifanc eu sêl –
Yr ifanc biau'r rhyfel,
Yn rhoi mwy i'r oriau mân,
Yn griw fyn grafu'r graean.

I ninnau'r ofnus, hynach,
Eto byth, agwedd plant bach
Sydd gan rhain; rhwydd eu heinioes,
Chwarae â'r her, heb ei chroes.
Oriau gwyllt, moriant 'I'r gad'
Yn ddiau, heb ddyhead.
Rhain a'u hachos un noson,
Rhain ddi-syfl, 'fory'n ddi-sôn!

       *   *   *

Y nos, er ei chynnau hi,
Daw tua dau eto i dewi,
Dim ond sibrydion tonnau
A nwydau bardd hyd y bae.

Hen eirch swrth drwy'r llewyrch sydd –
Lluniau o'r cychod llonydd,
A thrwy sawl cawell bellach
Edau fain y lleuad fach
Yn pwytho'r cameo i'r co'
Ac R.S. yn Garuso.

    *gweryru yw'r gair, eithr gwehyru ddywedir yn Llŷn.
    Gwehyru ddwedai R.S. hefyd.

Guarding

An old man dreaming melodies, their essence the sun, wind and rain. Yet from under a prickly blanket he saw the twilight of his people. Anguish in his voice, he was a metaphor of the sea, a caricature of its woe.

Neigwl's stallion waves in rhythm as he, the 'No one' he proclaimed to be, turned towards the warmth of the land. Tired of the freezing cold nights creaking with the glaciers of our history.

How the might of the waves, the alarm clock of the Atlantic thumped at his pillow each morning! Hovering, he watched like the seagull, a scowling eye at the cliff edge. We heard his trembling voice echoing over the bay, exploding against the surge. Fire in his tight lips, flames in his gaunt face.

In fear for our future, he chastised our heedlessness. Sometimes impatient, the pain obvious in his soul, his tongue pleaded for us, a stark warning in its wake.

In the rapids of his song, he was the wild rose and a whiff of rosemary in our nostrils. Listen to his lyric in the reeds by the shore, the man with those warm smiling eyes.

* * *

From his cold resting place he returns with the spray and the breeze to his old cottage, in time for dawn and the birds.

Those miracles in trees and sea melodies at Maen Melyn tuned to Llŷn's beauty.

Our language his hope, our culture his altar, a voice for a dumb nation, in tune with its high spirited young. Priest for their protest, grieving from the heart. Always, the act not the actor.

Sometimes imprisoned in campaigns, cold steel in his voice, but a warm sun to many. Bold as the men of Erin who turned plough-shares to arms, such was his concern for his people. Undeterred by press lenses laid in snares, untroubled by journalists preying; their fast and furious questions discharged with the velocity of gun barrels.

Breathing the power of the waves he strides along Porth Neigwl, frowning, while the wind beats the march of a secret army from the mountain. An old man justifying our existence, the waves his language. A face for the silent multitude, challenging that we stand with our young to close the breaches in our defences.

* * *

The night is alight! Young voices in the early hours, the shore alive with their dance, and in the waves, the passion of a poet. While the old lament for the past, unsure of the future, careful and suspicious of their protest.

* * *

A thin braid of moonlight weaving through the lobster pots reflects boats still as coffins. A beautiful, tranquil scene. RS, now gone, safe as Caruso.

(translation by Gareth Neigwl)

Gareth Neigwl and Myrddin ap Dafydd

Cywydd: Enwogrwydd

(RS y bardd)

Rhwng y lli a'r llwyni llus,
gardd gudd nid gardd gyhoeddus
fynasai o, llwyfan swil
i'r gân o'i ddaear gynnil.

Ond dôi at giât ei awen
griw llym am agor y llen:
y mae rhwyd mewn camerâu,
dan wn mewn rhai cwestiynau.

Troeai o'r tir tua'r tŷ,
glaw Neigwl yn ei wgu;
uwchlaw'r traeth ni chlywai'r trwch
o Lŷn waedd am lonyddwch.

Fame

(R.S. the poet)

Between the bay and the bilberry bushes, his choice would be a concealed garden for the shy unveiling of a poem in the barren soil.

But there arrived at his gate a stern crowd, possessed with delving into his world, camera shutters clicking their traps, questions fired through cocked pistols.

He turned to his cottage, Porth Neigwl's sweeping rain in his frown, but they were deaf to a cry from Llŷn, to be left alone.

(translation by Gareth Neigwl)

Oliver Reynolds

Thomases Two

Born in adjacent years
on the same friable coastline

one found England
a bad smell

(but was published
in London)

worshipped the clarity
of the frozen stream

and took for gospel
the claw marks of birds

the other marked his place in books
with rashers of bacon

lost the coating of his tongue
to a Vindaloo

(unpeeling it from his mouth
like a pink condom)

and sailed home from New York
in the Queen Elizabeth

the crew stacking his coffin
with whisky and wine

Owen Sheers

Inheritance

(After R.S. Thomas)

From my father a stammer
like a stick in the spokes of my speech.
A tired blink,
a need to have my bones
near the hill's bare stone.
An affection for the order of maps
and the chaos of bad weather.

From my mother
a sensitivity to the pain in the pleasure.
The eye's blue ore,
quiet moments beside a wet horse
drying in a rain-loud stable.
A joiner's lathe
turning fact into fable.

And from them both –
a desire for what they forged
in their shared lives;
testing it under the years' hard hammer,
red hot at its core,
cooled dark at its sides.

Daniel Tobin

A Stone in Aberdaron

The poem in the rock and
the poem in the mind
are not one...

– R. S. Thomas (1913-2000)

Driving the *Llŷn*, our tongues backed to teeth
Speaking the palette 'l' like Bushmen,
Soft click of a key sticking in language,
We navigate coastal roads in rain

Where the Atlantic shambles to Hell's Mouth
And Whistling Sands like wind-stanched pilgrims
Sped out of the past by some fleet machine
To this shearwater church on the Sound:

Your Sound, your church—an eyrie at the crux
Of the human village and the sea,
Ancient fields weathered into bracken, brine,
The membrane of this shingle shore,

Runnels of foam in the slow tidal hush.
Obstinate priest, rock-faced, you listened
For the presence of your God like a pulse
Thrumming in the offing's ashen verge,

Imagined Greetings

A whisper in the fleece of gunshot clouds.
Even now, chin deep in world, I love
Your raw vigil at the mirror's plunge,
Your rapt loneliness before the fathoms.

Here, under Hywyn's double nave, for years
You raised in faith the gleaming zero
Of the chalice rim. In the chancel's womb
You felt Christ like gritstone in the host.

For you the mind honed itself on this edge,
Your slate sublime hardened as a gem
Underground, resistant to thought, to song,
The threadbare scripts of keen equations,

Our vagrant shrines of the passing species,
And history pitiable as grass
Dunged by lost droves, while grace ran, a river
Disappearing down a swallow hole

To surface – your maker's rage, your longing –
In the depths: intimate immensity
That left you grim and brooding on the hills,
Your prayers signals beamed through shattered glass.

God was a raptor hunting you at night,
The brute vacuum portioned between stars,
Nameless well of sourceless light, sky's window,
And bone's rapture at the curtain's breath.

Your ashes scattered among these swells
Have mingled in the seething grottoes
Below bare cliffs, the seawall slicked green
As in some pre-Silurian dawn.

And there, in the scoured shallows, this stone
Big as a room, washed as if by microns
Ashore, bright-flecked, emerald, amazing.
We feel around it for the miracle

It is – rune of earth, capsule of pure time,
Lobe of the Godhead's adamantine brain.
What would you have conjured from the gift
As day's first bathers dive into the surf?

John Tripp

on hearing r. s. thomas

under splash
of cockpit floods,
grey peninsula priest
in off-peg grey suit
limp red tie
spare   anti-windbag
incantating like monk
cistercian bereft.

i yawn
bored
at the 15th tract,
exit   worrying
oddly depressed.
how much of that
dislocated prayer
god's torture in public
was true?
i move quick to the stiff
reinforcement of gin.

sour   bitter
unbending
country priest,
one of christ's
strange errand boys,
do you take weetabix dust
or porridge
to break your fast

or a dry windfall
welsh apple?

you see eternity in lightshaft
shooting through cloudgap
on a penful of sheep.
you defecate like me
cracked inside my skull
who sees at slow dusk
from the skeleton rot
the orange disc go down
across the nameless common.

Damian Walford Davies

Villanelle: The Hide

(i.m. R. S. Thomas)

Nightjars purr. Out of mind
all winter in the churrless air,
their burring stirs me in the hide.

This hutch is where the grind
of self on self cries off – where
nights won't jar; the mind

shuts down to nothing, just the wind,
and trains its lenses on rare
grasses stirring near the hide.

The reedbeds' camouflage has lied
before. Light stirs. There? There –
Mind in the crosshairs of the mind.

They found this ground by stars, aligned
with stars; the lure of here –
the thought expands inside the hide.

Goatsuckers, nighthawks, ride
the failing updraughts of this prayer.
That purr again. Out of mind
the burrless winters of the hide.

Jason Walford Davies

Cinio Gydag R. S.

(Gwahoddiad gan y bardd i ymuno ag ef am ginio
mewn tŷ bwyta ym Môn, 26 Gorffennaf 1995)

Nodyn: Yr oedd R. S. Thomas yn yrrwr arbennig o gyflym.

> He is such a fast
> God, always before us and
> leaving as we arrive.
> (R. S. Thomas, 'Pilgrimages')

Llanfair-yng-Nghornwy, a'r croeso'n heulog
yn ei dŷ uwchben y weilgi, y dŵr fel pali.

Yna'n sydyn ganddo: 'Nid trwy weddi'n
unig y bydd byw dyn'. Gwên, a'i ên yn crynu'n

arab. 'Dilynwch fi', dywedodd, a neidio
i'r Honda Civic gwrthddinesig

y codai'r haf ei hun ohono'n
donnau gwresog ger y môr ym Môn.

Gallwn dyngu, gan mor hyglyw'r sŵn
gweryru yn yr injan, iddo dyrchu

ysbardunau i ystlysau'r car
(rhyddiaith bur i fardd mor fawr

yw troed ar sbardun). Ac nid 'car'
ychwaith, ond 'cerbyd' oedd ei ddewis

derm, gan beri imi'i weld bob tro
y cydiai'i acen yng ngwar y gair –

ac yntau'n llaeswallt a Silwraidd,
yn llawnarfog â llên –

fel Caradawg o gerbydwr ar y maes.
Ac yn y cerbyd, cymryd y goes,

a heuliau goleuadau'r groes-
ffordd yn enigma iddo, yn god

i'w dorri ar y daith. Oferedd
oedd ceisio cwrso: roedd yn fardd

mor gyflym – o hyd o'n blaenau,
ac yn gadael yr holl bentrefi,

yr holl blwyfi syfrdan, cyn inni
gyrraedd. Tynnai'i sgilwynt Fôn ei hun

i'w ganlyn, yn llain lanio
oes o ehediadau. Ac ar hap

y gwelsom yr Honda hwnnw'n
torheulo mewn maes parcio, ei arian

byw yn haul ei hun. Gwên gan y bardd
o weld fforddolion blin, a'i ên

yn crynu'n arab eto: 'Ble fuoch chi
gyhyd?' Ac weithiau, o glywed

nodau gleision seiren ganol nos,
daw'r cof am ras dros ddaear Môn,

am fardd a'i farch Rhiannon
o Honda arian, ac am ystyr hud

Effaith Doppler ei fyw a'i Fod.

Lunch with R. S.

(An invitation to join the poet for lunch in a restaurant on Anglesey, 26 July 1995)

Note: R. S. Thomas was an especially fast driver.

> He is such a fast
> God, always before us and
> leaving as we arrive.
>   (R. S. Thomas, 'Pilgrimages')

Llanfair-yng-Nghornwy, the welcome sunny
in his house above the ocean, the water's silk brocade.

Then, out of the blue: 'Man shall not live
by prayer alone'. A smile, his chin a witty

quiver. 'Follow me', he said, leaping
into the Honda Civic (an indulged nod

to cities), from which the very summer rose
in waves of heat by the sea in Môn.

I could have sworn, so loud the sound
of neighing from the engine, that he'd kicked

spurs into the car's sides (a foot on an accelerator
is mere prose for so great a maker).

Not 'car', either; his chosen term was 'chariot':
I saw as much each time his accent chose

to take that word and shake it by its neck –
this long-haired Silurian, bristling

with verse, a Caractacus of a charioteer
in the field. And in the chariot, forever taking

flight, the suns of traffic-lights at cross-
roads an enigma to him – a code

to be broken on the journey. Futile
our giving chase: he was such a fast

poet, always ahead, and leaving an island's
villages – its reeling parishes – behind

before we'd even arrived. And pulled in his slip-
stream, the whole of Anglesey – a landing strip

of a lifetime's flights. And by chance it was
we saw that Honda sunbathing

in a car park, its silver the quick-
silver of the sun itself. Seeing wayfarers

worn-out, the poet smiled, his chin again
a witty quiver: 'What took you so long?'.

And sometimes, on hearing a siren's notes
at night – a bruising blue on black – the memory

returns of a post haste chase across
an island's earth, of a silver Honda

that became Rhiannon's horse.
Uncanny, the Doppler Effect

of a god, of a poet, passing.

(translation by Jason Walford Davies)

John Powell Ward

A Bride in White

(Justin Wintle, *Furious Interiors* page 363)

Carried over the threshold
As before, a bride in white
But as to the hair this time,
The snowfalls of age
For her final honeymoon.
'OK, you have her'
The poet said to Death,
The wound in his side,
The hole whence Adam's rib
Was taken and still not healed.

It says here that Thomas
Home from an operation
For hernia still managed
To carry his dying Elsi
From the car to the cottage
When both were gone eighty.
I bet she looked and laughed,
His love still ferocious
At such most grievous loss
Which none of the poems filled.

Harri Webb

The Next Village to Manafon

It was half-past seven on a Saturday night
When we stopped off at The Powys Arms.
Already the locals were half-way tight,
Red-faced men from the steep green farms.

Some talked of girls and country pleasures
And some were grumbling about the hay
And some were discussing the bardic measures,
Heirs of Owain Cyfeiliog they.

We kept our end up, passing strangers,
As best we could, with what tales we knew,
Avoiding the subtle verbal dangers
Laid like poachers by the deft-tongued crew.

Song for song we joined in the singing
And not for a moment the clonc did flag,
The glasses clinked and the room was ringing.
I hope God drinks, said the village wag.

It was half-past nine on Saturday night
As we broke the spell and drove over the hill.
They pressed us to stay, but we took our flight
And none too soon, or we'd be there still.

Ianto Rhydderch: Tch Tch

One day while I was docking swedes
With a slow moronic grin
And all my ancestors' misdeeds
Wrought their sour death within,

Suddenly there came into view
A figure gaunt and tall.
He said, Forgive me naming you.
I made no sound at all.

He carried on at tedious length
About my life so grim,
It took all my idiot peasant strength
To be polite to him.

At last he ceased and strode away,
The cold Welsh rain came down,
In puddles in that barren clay
I watched my country drown.

Then, indistinguishable from mud,
I started my old car,
The sickness of my tainted blood
Inclined me to a jar.

And oh what festering itch of sin
Brought this damp thought to me
As I fuddled in a squalid inn:
Un bain't much help to we.

Daniel Westover

At Porth Neigwl

No nearer than this;
So that I can see their shapes,
And know them human
But not who they are.

– R. S. Thomas, 'On the Shore'

Close enough to name what is here—
    broken jar, paintbrush handle,
    beer can, pink and blue
    tangle of rope, glove,
    newspaper, milk carton,
    bin bag snapping in the wind,
    yogurt pot, headless doll
    caught in a piece of netting—
I think about a poet's barriers.
Half offered by the landscape, half fashioned
with his words, the protective walls
kept actual Wales away
and imagined Wales away from human hands.
His dream required distance. Too close,
we soiled it with our breath.
He queried a farmer, a country, a God,
but none stepped through the gap
of hedge or cloud. When we came too near,
he choked on our exhaust.
Leaving the groomed grass of St. James's Park,
half his ticket in hand, he posted
his own sign: *Have a care.*

His heart's pastures needed fencing.
His poems were the bread and wine
he offered the distant faces on the shore,
and I hear their music once again
as I stand at Hell's Mouth, among the waste
of what he could not love.

Rowan Williams

Deathship

in memory of R S Thomas

The last years, words from a window
smoothing the sea, the iron back and forth
to probe the fugitive wrinkles
carving a path down to the lost gate.

What hid in the pale clefts till now
feels for the light, a soft uncertain
fingering as if through
stone, through furrows of flint.

The tides pressed neat as for an evening out:
time to drag down a black boat from the shed,
off through the gate, to balance
on the slow sea at dark, ready to sail.

The smoke will rise, the cloudy pillar
wavering across the sky's long page
At dawn, somewhere westward,
the boat flares in a blaze of crying birds.

John Wood

Two Poems Inspired by M. E. Eldridge

for Gwydion

1. Skulls and Talons

Down thin Lleyn roads above Hell's Mouth
he'd put out a flag on a fishing pole
to catch our attention. We talked
of his work, his tastes. Later his wife,
aging, still beautiful–her face shimmering
like a girl's in the silvery film of a daguerreotype–
made tea. "China or India," she asked.
And we had both, ate the scones and bara brith
she'd made, the jam from small plums he'd picked.
She showed us her drawings of birds, intricate,
minute studies. Smiling, she said "They ask me
if I kill them." On a table across from us
lay an owl he'd found for her. One of her paintings
was of her hands when she was ill. "I only had
my hands to look at then." She kept insisting us
to more sweets. The hickory smelling fire burned
in their cottage, and we talked of Wales' calm war–
"sure to be lost" and "where wrongs made
no rights." "The English are very dirty,"
she said. "Wales' sands are strewn with papers
that held their chips." When he preached
at Abadaron they'd hang their clothes
on grave stones and dress in rubber
to see what tried to go beneath
waters they fouled. She had placed

shells, the skulls of birds about the room,
round stones from a river next the parsonage
where they first lived. She showed us
Gwydion's portrait, and we thought of "trout
from the green river." She moved slowly
as stones in a river might move. She painted
skulls and talons. We thought we knew why.

2. Feathers and Bones

"What can I do–sit at the border
with a gun and shoot them
as they drive their caravans in?
Filthy people! How could I
have married one?" said with
some humor. "And, yes,
they even hang bathing suits
on the gravestones to dry."
In his study we sat
by a window–rat and rabbit
skulls aglow on the dustless sill.
"Not a poem in it," he said,
as he threw Ashbury's
new book hard to the floor.
I suggested a trip to the US
with venues and good money
I could arrange. "You sound
like an American car salesman.
[But what did he know of Americans
or their car salesmen?] I'm always
being told the same: 'Come down
to London. I can promise
an audience of five hundred' as if

one Englishman wasn't enough—
much less five hundred!" At tea
she seemed to gentle him,
and our talk turned.

Later, as we drove from Wales,
we continued to think of them
even as years passed, on them still
in their immaculate, whitewashed rooms
sitting among the bones and feathers
her sure, steady hand enlivened.

Contributors

While this anthology was in the proofreading stage, I learned that one of the most distinguished contributors – Tony Conran – had passed away in Ysbyty Gwynedd in Bangor. I met Tony at his home in 1975, where he treated me – an aspiring poet visiting from America – with great kindness and generosity. All those involved with Welsh literature and culture will miss his creativity and his passion.

David Lloyd, January 2013

Dannie Abse is a poet, fiction writer, playwright and memoirist. He has written and edited more than sixteen books of poetry. His most recent novel, *The Strange Case of Dr Simmonds & Dr Glas*, was published in 2002 (Robson). His most recent poetry collection, *Two for Joy: Scenes from Married Life*, appeared in 2010 (Hutchison).

Myrddin ap Dafydd is a Welsh-language poet who won the National Chair (for strict metre poetry) at the 1990 and 2002 Eisteddfodau. He was the first Bardd Plant Cymru (Poet Laureate for Children in Wales) in 2000; his fifth collection of verse was published in 2012; and he is the publisher and owner of Gwasg Carreg Gwalch.

Elin ap Hywel is a poet, translator and editor who works in Welsh and English. Her poetry collections include *Pethau Brau* (Y Lolfa, 1982) and *Ffiniau/Borders*, co-authored with Grahame Davies (Gomer, 2002).

Roy Ashwell is the author of three books of poems, with his next collection, *The Garden*, appearing in 2013. His poems have appeared in numerous poetry magazines in the UK and the USA. He serves as poetry editor of the web journal *In Between*, and is the founder of the London Poetry Circle.

Bryan Aspden (1933–1999) is the author of two collections of poetry: *News of the Changes* (Seren, 1984 – winner of the Welsh Arts Council's first New Poets Competition) and *Blind Man's Meal* (Seren, 1989).

Ruth Bidgood lives in mid-Wales. Her collection *Time Being* (Seren, 2009) won the Roland Mathias Prize 2011 and was a Poetry Book Society Recommendation. Cinnamon Press recently published her new collection *Above the Forests*. Matthew Jarvis' study of her poetry in the 'Writers of Wales' series (University of Wales Press) has also just been published.

Jane Blank is a novelist, poet, dramatist, script writer, and tutor in creative writing whose mother's family is from Eglwys Fach. She now lives in Abergavenny, where she teaches English and Drama in a Welsh-language school. Her novel *The Geometry of Love* appeared in 2009 (Y Lolfa).

Gillian Clarke has been the National Poet of Wales since 2008. She was awarded the Queen's Gold Medal for Poetry in 2010 and the Wilfred Owen Award in 2012, and she is a member of the Gorsedd y Beirdd, Eisteddfod Genedlaethol, Wrecsam, 2011. Recent books include a prose collection, *At the Source* (2008), and the poetry collections, *A Recipe for Water* (2009) and *Ice* (2012), all from Carcanet.

Tony Conran (1931-2013) from Bangor is well known as a poet, translator and critic. His recent poetry publications include *Red Sap of Love* (2006) and *What Brings You Here So Late* (2008) both published by Gwasg Carreg Gwalch. His translations include *Welsh Verse* (Seren, 1992) and *Peacemakers* (Gomer, 1997). His work has been performed by the Conran Poetry Chorus/Corws Cerddi Conran.

John Davies lives in Prestatyn where he is a woodcarver and extra-mural English tutor. He has worked in Michigan and in

Washington State, and has lectured in poetry at Brigham Young University in the USA. He has edited several anthologies. His most recent poetry collection is *North by South* (Seren, 2003).

William Virgil Davis is Professor of English and Writer-in-Residence at Baylor University in Waco, Texas and the author of numerous books of criticism and poetry, including *Landscape and Journey*, winner of the 2009 New Criterion Poetry Prize and the Helen C. Smith Memorial Award for Poetry.

Jon Dressel is the American-born grandson of Welsh emigrants. From 1973 to 1998 he directed the American Programme and later the MA in Creative Writing at Trinity College Carmarthen. He has published six volumes of poetry and won prizes in major competitions in both the USA and the UK.

Menna Elfyn is an award-winning poet and playwright, and the author of twelve collections of poetry. Her most recent, *Murmur* (Bloodaxe Books, 2012), was selected as the first Poetry Book Society Recommended Translation. Her work has been translated into eighteen languages, receiving an International Foreign Poetry Prize in 2009. A *Western Mail* columnist since 1994, she is also Director of Creative Writing at the University of Wales, Trinity Saint David.

Peter Finch is a literary entrepreneur, poet and psycho-geographer living in Cardiff. Until recently he was Chief Executive of Academi (later Literature Wales). He now writes full time. His recent books include *Selected Later Poems* and *Zen Cymru* (Seren) and the Real Cardiff series. His new book about the Severn estuary, *Edging The Estuary*, is due from Seren in 2013.

Greg Hill was editor of *The Anglo-Welsh Review*. He is a regular contributor of poetry and critical articles to Welsh literary journals. His poetry collections include *Bastard Englyns* (Nant, 2000).

Jeremy Hooker is an English poet and critic living in Wales, where he is Emeritus Professor of the University of Glamorgan. His ten volumes of poetry are substantially represented in *The Cut of the Light: Poems 1965–2005* (Enitharmon, 2006). His other books include *Welsh Journal* (Seren, 2001).

Emyr Humphreys is a poet and novelist with over twenty books published, including *The Taliesin Tradition* (a cultural history of Wales, Black Raven Press, 1983), *Collected Poems* (University of Wales Press, 1999), and a short story collection, *The Woman at the Window* (Seren, 2010). This anthology's title is taken, with permission, from Humphreys' poem 'S. L. i R. S. (An Imagined Greeting)'.

Mark Jarman's latest collection of poetry is *Bone Fires: New and Selected Poems* (Sarabande, 2011). He is Centennial Professor of English at Vanderbilt University and lives in Nashville, TN, USA.

Mike Jenkins won the Wales Book of the Year in 1998 for his short story collection *Wanting To Belong*. His latest book of poetry is *Moor Music* (Seren, 2010). Next year his new collection of poems and stories in Merthyr dialect, *Barkin!*, will be published by Gwasg Carreg Gwalch. He serves as co-editor of the poetry magazine *Red Poets*.

T. H. Jones (1921–1965) was the author of five poetry collections, all from Rupert Hart-Davies: *The Enemy in the Heart* (1957), *Songs of a Mad Prince* (1960), *The Beast at the Door* (1963), *The Colour of Cockcrowing* (posthumous, 1966) and *The Collected Poems of T. Harri Jones* (1977).

Rupert M. Loydell is Senior Lecturer in English with Creative Writing at University College Falmouth and the editor of *Stride* and *With* magazines. He is the author of many books of poetry, including *Wildlife* (Shearsman, 2011) and the artist's book-in-a-box *The Tower of Babel* (Like This Press, 2012). He has also co-authored several collaborative works, and edited anthologies for Salt, Shearsman, Knives, Forks & Spoons, and Stride.

Roland Mathias (1915–2000) was a poet, critic, editor, and author of eight poetry collections, including *The Collected Poems of Roland Mathias* (edited by Sam Adams, University of Wales Press, 2000).

John Mole lives in Hertfordshire and for many years taught there and ran The Mandeville Press with Peter Scupham. His most recent publications are *The Point of Loss* (Enitharmon, 2011) and an online English/Romanian selection, *The Memory of Gardens*, from Bucharest's Contemporary Literature Press. His collection of poems for children, *All the Frogs*, appeared as the second title in Salt's Children's Poetry Library in 2010.

Twm Morys is a poet and singer from Llanystumdwy in Eifionydd, north Wales. The song 'Y Sŵn' ('The Sound'), which he sings with his band, Bob Delyn a'r Ebillion, is in part a tribute to R.S. Thomas. His most recent poetry collection is 2, from Cyfoeddiadau Barddas. He won the National Chair (for strict metre poetry) at the 2003 Eisteddfod.

Oliver Reynolds was born in Cardiff in 1957. *Hodge*, his fifth book of poetry, was published in 2010. He lives in London and works as an usher at the Royal Opera House.

Owen Sheers is a poet, author, and scriptwriter. He has published two poetry collections, *The Blue Book* and *Skirrid Hill*, which won a Somerset Maugham Award. His debut prose work, a non-fiction narrative set in Zimbabwe titled *The Dust Diaries*, won the Welsh Book of the Year 2005. Sheers published a novel, *Resistance*, in 2008 and a novella, *White Ravens*, in 2009.

Daniel Tobin's latest book of poems, *Belated Heavens*, won the Massachusetts Book Award in Poetry. A collection of essays, *Awake* *in America,* is newly out from the University of Notre Dame Press. Among his awards are fellowships from the National Endowment for the Arts and the John Simon Guggenheim Foundation.

John Tripp (1927–1986) was a short-story writer and poet, and a gifted performer of his work. He served as literary editor of *Planet: the Welsh Internationalist* during the 1970s. The author of many volumes of poetry, his *Collected Poems* was published in 1978.

Damian Walford Davies is the author of the poetry collections *Whiteout* (with Richard Marggraf Turley; Parthian, 2006), *Suit of Lights* (Seren, 2009) and *Witch* (Seren, 2012). He is currently editing *R. S. Thomas: Poems to Elsi* for Seren. He is Head of the Department of English and Creative Writing at Aberystwyth University.

Jason Walford Davies is Senior Lecturer in the School of Welsh, and Co-Director of the R.S. Thomas Study Centre, at Bangor University. He is the editor and translator of *R. S. Thomas: Autobiographies* (Dent, 1997), the author of a monograph on the poet's indebtedness to the Welsh literary tradition, *Gororau'r Iaith* (University of Wales Press, 2003), and the editor of *R.S. Thomas: Letters to Raymond Garlick 1951–1999* (Gomer, 2009). He is currently co-editing R.S. Thomas' uncollected poems for Bloodaxe Books.

John Powell Ward is an Honorary Research Fellow at the University of Wales, Swansea. His *Selected and New Poems* appeared from Seren in 2004. His portfolio *Poetry or Type* was exhibited at the Hay Poetry Jamboree in 2012. His critical study *The Poetry of R.S. Thomas* appeared in 2001 (Seren).

Harri Webb (1920–1994) wrote verse, ballads and journalism that were 'unashamedly nationalistic'. He began as a Welsh Republican and ended as a left-wing activist in the ranks of Plaid

Cymru. By profession a librarian, he lived, for the most part, in Merthyr Tydfil and Cwm-bach in the Cynon Valley, and died in his home city of Swansea. His *Collected Poems*, edited by Meic Stephens, was published in 1995 (Gomer).

Daniel Westover's poetry has appeared widely in American journals and anthologies, including *North American Review* and *The Southern Poetry Anthology*. He is author of *R. S. Thomas: A Stylistic Biography* (University of Wales, 2011) and is currently writing a biography of Leslie Norris (Parthian). He lives in Johnson City, Tennessee.

Gareth Neigwl was born and bred on the Llŷn peninsula. After his college days he returned to his roots to live and work. He started writing poetry, mostly in cynghanedd (strict metre) during his mid thirties. A collection of his poems, *Ar y Tir Mawr, Cerddi Gareth Neigwl*, was recently published by Gwasg Carreg Gwalch.

Rowan Williams is a theologian, translator, poet, and the former Archbishop of Canterbury – now Lord Williams of Oystermouth, Master of Magdalene College, Cambridge. His collection, *The Poems of Rowan Williams* (Perpetua, 2002), was long-listed for the Wales Book of the Year award.

John Wood received the Gold Deutscher Fotobuchpreis for his collection of poems *Endurance and Suffering* (Galerie Vevais, 2009) and the Iowa Poetry Prize of the University of Iowa Press for *In Primary Light* (1993) and also for *The Gates of the Elect Kingdom* (1996). His *Selected Poems 1968–1998* was published in 1999 (University of Arkansas Press) and *The Fictions of History* in 2011 (privately printed).

Acknowledgements

I want to thank the following for their advice and support: Myrddin ap Dafydd, John Bollard, Tony Brown, Margaret Lloyd, Jen Llywelyn, Meic Stephens, Kim Waale, Jason Walford Davies. I am also indebted to the United States Fulbright Program for my fellowship at Bangor University, Wales, home of the R. S. Thomas Study Centre, where the idea for this anthology originated; and to the Research and Development Committee of Le Moyne College, for a grant and a sabbatical leave in support of this project. I am grateful to Myrddin ap Dafydd for help selecting the poems in Welsh.

Dannie Abse: 'Is Creation a Destructive Force?' was previously published in *Poetry Wales*.

Elin ap Howell: 'The Stranger' (translation of Menna Elfyn's 'Titw Tomos') is from *Perfect Blemish/Perffaith Nam* (Bloodaxe).

Roy Ashwell: 'R.S. Writes His Biography in a New Tongue' was previously published in *David Jones Journal*.

Bryan Aspden: 'Travellers in the Dream Trade' was previously published in *Poetry Wales*.

Ruth Bidgood: 'Bereft' is from *New and Selected Poems* (Seren).

Jane Blank: 'R. S. Thomas in Eglwys Fach' is from *Naked Playing the Cello* (The Collective Press).

Gillian Clarke: 'The Poet' (translation of Menna Elfyn's 'Y Bardd Di-flewyn') and 'Handkerchief Kiss' (translation of Menna Elfyn's 'Cusan Hances') are from *Cusan Dyn Dall/Blind Man's Kiss* (Bloodaxe); 'RS' is from *Making the Beds for the Dead* (Carcanet).

Tony Conran: 'The Great R. S. is Gone' is from *Red Sap of Love* (Gwasg Carreg Gwalch).

John Davies: 'R.S. Thomas' was previously published in *Poetry Wales*.

William Virgil Davis: 'First Light' is from *Landscape and Journey* (New Criterion Series); 'The Island' was published in *The New Criterion*.

Jon Dressel: all poems are from *Out of Wales: Fifty Poems 1973–1983* (Alun Books)

Menna Elfyn: 'Y Bardd di-flewyn' and 'Cusan Hances' are from *Cusan Dyn Dall/Blind Man's Kiss* (Bloodaxe); 'Titw Tomos' is from *Perfect Blemish/Perffaith Nam* (Bloodaxe)

Peter Finch: 'A Welsh Wordscape' is from *Selected Poems* (Poetry Wales Press); 'Well-Proportioned Panorama' is from *Food* (Seren); 'Hills' is from *Poems For Ghosts* (Seren); 'R S Visits The City' is published by permission of the author; 'The Light' is from www.peterfinch.com; 'RNLD TOMOS' is from *Useful* (Seren).

Greg Hill: 'R.S. Th.' was previously published in *Planet*.

Jeremy Hooker: 'In the Footsteps of No-One' is from *The Cut of the Light* (Enitharmon Press).

Emyr Humphreys: 'S.L. i R.S. (An Imagined Greeting)' is from *Collected Poems* (University of Wales Press).

Mark Jarman: 'R. S. Thomas' is from *Bone Fires: New and Selected Poems* (Sarabande Books).

Mike Jenkins: 'Places You Cannot Go' was previously published in *Quantum Leap*.

T. H. Jones: 'Back?' is from *Collected Poems* (Gomer).

Rupert M. Loydell: 'Even in Darkness: i.m. R. S. Thomas' was previously published in *The David Jones Journal*.

Roland Mathias: 'Sir Gelli to R. S.' is from *Collected Poems* (University of Wales Press).

John Mole: 'Eh?' is from *Depending on the Light* (Peterloo Poets).

Twm Morys: 'R.S.' is from *2* (Cyhoeddiadau Barddas).

Oliver Reynolds: 'Thomases Two' is from *Hodge* (Areté Books).

Owen Sheers: 'Inheritance' is from *Skirrid Hill* (Seren).

Dan Tobin: 'A Stone in Aberdaron' was previously published in *Hudson Review*.

John Tripp: 'on hearing r. s. thomas' was previously published in *Second Aeon*.

Damian Walford Davies: 'Villanelle: The Hide' is published by permission of the author.

Jason Walford Davies: 'Cinio Gydag R.S.' was previously published in *Barddas*.

John Powell Ward: 'A Bride in White' is from *New and Selected Poems* (Cinnamon).

Harri Webb: 'The Next Village to Manafon' and 'Ianto Rhydderch: Tch Tch' are from *Collected Poems* (Gomer).

Daniel Westover: 'At Porth Neigwl' is by permission of the author.

Rowan Williams: 'Deathship' is from *The Poems of Rowan Williams* (Perpetua).

John Wood: 'Two Poems Inspired by M. E. Eldridge' is published by permission of the author.